# Susan Perl's
# Human Body Book

By Leslie McGuire

Platt & Munk, Publishers / New York

A Division of Grosset & Dunlap

## YOU AND YOUR BODY

Every day you do things, you see things, you taste things, you touch things, and you smell things. Sometimes you run, and sometimes you sneeze. Some of the things you do with your body you do on purpose, and some of them just happen. The body is a very special piece of machinery. Each part helps all the other parts, and all together they are what makes you the person that you are. Even though not everyone is the same, and even though everyone likes to do things their own way, everyone's body works the same way.

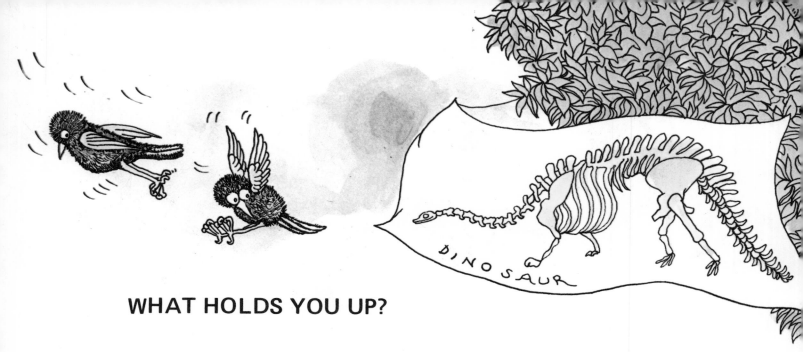

DINOSAUR

## WHAT HOLDS YOU UP?

Your skeleton is the frame that holds up your body. It also protects all the soft inside parts that make your body work. The skeleton is made up of lots of bones. Some are very big, like your leg bones, and some are very small, like your finger bones. Each place where your bones join together is called a joint. Every joint bends, and that's why you can move around and do things. A joint is your knee, or your wrist, or your elbow. Sometimes your elbow is called your funny bone. It isn't really a funny bone, but sometimes when you hit your elbow, it gives your whole arm a funny tingly feeling.

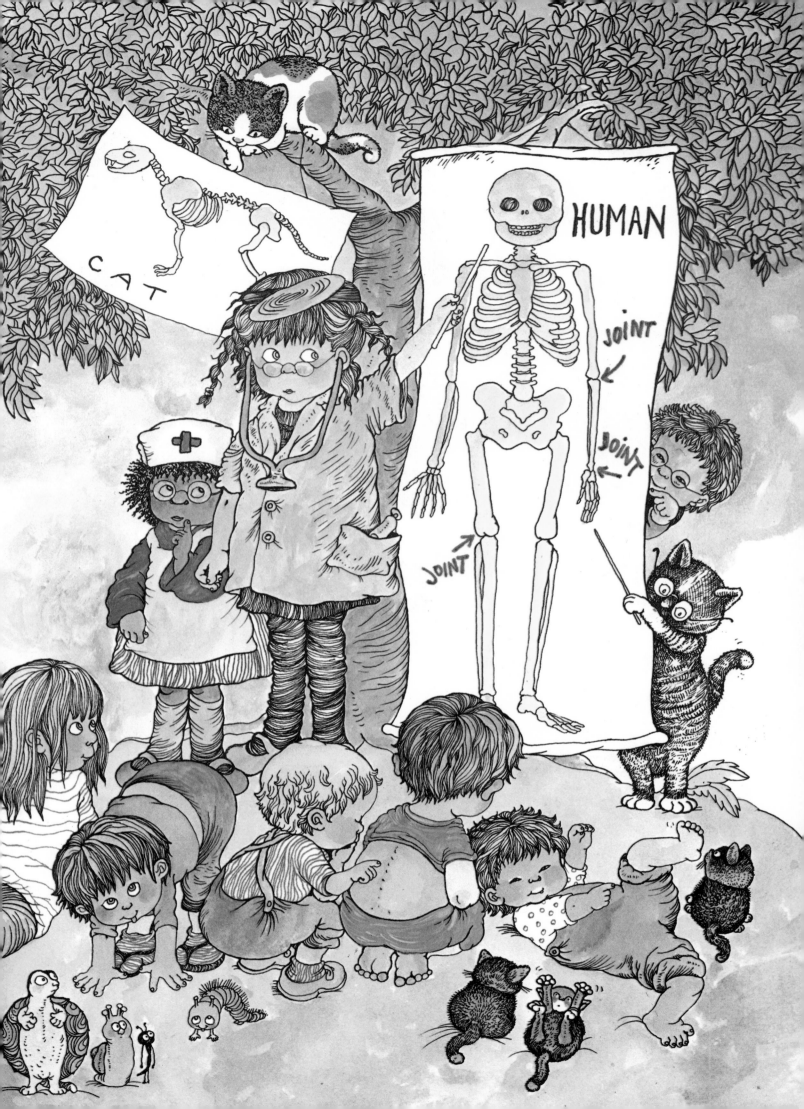

## WHAT HOLDS YOU TOGETHER AND MAKES YOU MOVE?

Muscles make you move and also hold all your bones together. When you want to bend over and pick up something, muscles move you over, bend you down, curl your fingers around what you want, and then straighten you up again. You use your muscles every time you move. Your muscles help give you a shape, too, and they help people know how you feel. When you smile, the muscles in your face pull up the corners of your lips. When you frown, they pull down your eyebrows and the corners of your lips, too. You can look happy or grumpy or worried or angry, and the muscles of the face will show it. Muscles help you play, and work, and even stand on your head if you want. But standing on your head takes practice.

## YOUR SKIN COVERS YOU ALL OVER.

Your skin is your outside covering. It is the first thing you see when you look at your body. It is waterproof and air can't get through it. It protects you from germs, and it also tells you when you are hot or cold, and even when you are cut. Your skin covers you, protects you, and warns you about lots of things. It tells you if things are rough or smooth, dry or wet.

Skin comes in different colors. Some is very light, and some
is very dark. Some is a shade in between. The color of your
skin is a result of the amount of pigment you have. All
skin pigment *is* some shade of brown. That is why you never
see anyone who is white as a sheet, or black as night, or yellow
as buttercups. The more pigment people have, the darker their
skin is; the less pigment they have, the lighter their skin is. But
all people are the same inside, no matter what color their skin is.

## WHERE DO YOU DO ALL YOUR THINKING?

You do all your thinking with your brain. Your brain is inside your head, and it is completely enclosed by a bone called the skull. This protects it. Your brain is what receives all the messages from the outside world, puts them in order, and tells you what to do about them. Your brain is what makes you remember things, or have dreams, or make up stories. It also does a lot of things that you don't have to think about. For example, it keeps your heart beating, and it makes you breathe, and it takes care of digesting all your food when you eat. Your brain is really what keeps you alive, and also what makes being alive so very interesting.

## WHAT HAPPENS TO YOUR FOOD ONCE YOU EAT IT?

Once you have chewed up your food, you swallow it, and it goes down inside your tummy. That is where it is digested. Once it is completely digested, it goes into your bloodstream, and all the proteins and vitamins and minerals go to all parts of your body and help you to grow, and play, and do all the things you like to do.

The parts of the food that you don't need stay in your bloodstream until they are ready to leave your body. Your body is working all the time digesting food that you eat. That's why you feel so sleepy after a great big dinner. Your body has to work extra hard to digest all that food.

## WHY DO YOU BREATHE ALL THE TIME?

Everybody needs oxygen to stay alive. When you breathe in air, your lungs clean it, and the oxygen in the air goes into little sacs. Here the blood vessels can pick it up and carry it to every part of your body along with the digested food that you have eaten. When you breathe out, the part of the air that you don't need, called carbon dioxide, comes out. You breathe in and out all day long because your body needs fresh oxygen in order to keep working all the time. Usually you breathe in and out about eighteen times a minute, but if you jump up and down, or run around in circles, you breathe much faster. That's because you need more oxygen when you use up energy.

## WHAT MAKES THAT THUMPING NOISE IN YOUR CHEST?

That thumping noise in your chest is made by your heart. Your heart is a very important pump that pushes the blood through all your blood vessels, all around your body. This is the way that every part of your body gets nourishment and oxygen. Your blood vessels are like special plumbing pipes that carry your blood all around your body and back to your heart. Your heart beats all the time, even when you're sound asleep. Your heart looks almost like your closed fist. Valentines are supposed to look like hearts but they really don't. Valentines are very pretty, of course, much prettier than your heart is, but not anywhere near as useful.

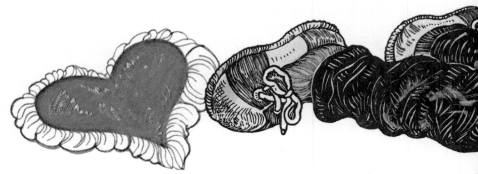